MEDITATIONS

OF A COMMON MAN
AND HIS EXTRAORDINARY DAUGHTER

A series of poetic snapshots of life from the different vantage points

of a father and his daughter

Craig and Whitney Pandil

CONTENTS

Inspiration

Craig's Work

Whitney's Work

Inspiration

My life has been shaped by the hands of many different people, and forged on life's anvil by the events of day-to-day living. Some events and personalities have naturally allowed themselves to become very important to me as time moves on. Earlier in my life, I learned the importance of letting others know how much they meant to me, but was restrained from actually telling them due to an introverted disposition. Age (or foolishness) seems to have given me some courage to bare my soul and accept the risks in doing so. Writing has allowed me out of that shell a little, and to say the things needed to those closest to me.

You know who you are.

Be it time shared with me, encouragement in difficult times, friendship or love, I thank you for your contributions to my life.

Craig

A Journey With Powerful Words

Not so long ago, I discovered a parallel in my life. It involved the history of God's Word, spoken at first, then its development into a written language, and my life-long lessons in learning its secrets. To some this may sound strange, but I find fascinating correlations of theology, history, the concept of time, and the learning process of the individual.

Before the development of the written word, the history of God and His people was passed from generation to generation in stories, told often to become ingrained in their culture. Eventually, the need arose to record this history and thus were born the picture-words called cunieform. The Greeks combined them into words and sentences to create koine. As other languages developed, translations were made, and The Word spread. Written now in Hebrew, too, this and the Greek version became the foundations for more translations into Arabic, German, English, and the hundreds of other tongues today.

My history parallels this same method, for I too, was introduced to the Word of God through stories long before I could read. Soon after followed a children's Bible filled with color reproductions of religious artwork as well as ink sketches in the margins. Although unable yet to read, those pictures ignited my imagination! They added reality and a permanence to the stories I'd heard just as the first cunieform picture-words must have done for others during the infancy of writing.

The parallels continue throughout my journey, with periodic stops for memorable snapshots. As a youth staying overnight at Grandma's house, I remember listening from the warmth of my bed in another room as she read passages from the Bible to my Grandpa. I sometimes wondered why he didn't just read them silently to himself, but now understand that this nightly ritual nourished not only him, but me as well.

School taught me to read and write. As my skills developed and I ventured into adolescence, I acquired an interest in calligraphy. Opportunities for using it seemed slim, but the death of one of my parent's closest friends offered just that. In a show of support and sympathy, I penned a short Bible verse on some posterboard for his widow, and in return received a lesson in the power of those words. Although neither matted nor framed, it hung in her bedroom for many years until it was too tattered to stay on the wall.

Illness and death draw us to The Word for comfort and understanding. The importance of this lesson was reinforced to me as my own mother struggled with her terminal illness, and I watched her dependence on the Bible for strength grow as her body weakened. Her continuing journey relies on those Powerful Words.

I find it fascinating to think of the time it took for these ancient events to unfold, and yet how quickly they repeat themselves within the short time span of a single lifetime. And the parallels continue. That childhood Bible has now been passed on to my son. As he enters adolescence, I see him reading it occasionally. *Guideposts* magazine comes as a gift from Grandma. And I continue to read those powerful words.

Some might think I write beautiful prose, and wonder from where such inspiration comes. It's simple really….I write from the heart, and walk this journey with Powerful Words.

Those Eyes

It began when her eyes met mine for the first time.

I haven't a clue what she saw or what she thought, or even why she looked my way. Perhaps it was noise, a movement. Maybe it was deliberate, maybe just a chance of fate. Did she catch me sweeping the faces of the others who were there? Or was I staring at her and hoping she'd find my gaze? As the people between us began melting away, I felt her eyes look past the physical and question my soul.

Is it you? Are you the one?

Her eyes were all I could see. Beautifully intense mirrors of green, they probed without touching, asked without speaking. I don't know what my eyes said to hers, but the answers must have been fine, and we began to talk. The time passed quickly, and soon it was time to go. I left, knowing I would see her again.

Not long after, those eyes met mine again. Lovely green eyes with flecks of gold, happy to see me again. We talked, but her eyes are all I remember. More familiar this time, they returned to my soul and sought answers to the same questions.

Is it you? Are you the one? Are you what is missing to make me whole? I wondered if my eyes were asking the same of hers. The time passed quickly, and again it was time to go.

Either by plan or by chance, we found ourselves at the same functions more often than not. Our conversation became more frequent. Talks soon led to walks, and more time to answer those emerald eyes.

Is it you? Are you the one?

It was on one of those walks that it happened. It was one of the simplest acts, very innocent, yet one of those eye-blink moments that become etched in the photos of a life, and define what it will be. As we walked, she slipped her hand into mine, and again those gorgeous eyes spoke to my soul.

It IS you! You ARE the one!

That simple touch confirmed the answers to the questions. A kiss sealed the bonding of two hearts. Difficult times lie ahead, but we would survive them as one, because the soul can not lie to the eyes, and loving touch speaks for the heart.

It began when her eyes first met mine. It continues as long as my soul can see.

With You

I was searching for a friend one day
And I found one in you
I went searching for acceptance
And found it with you
I wanted to search for tomorrow
And to look for it with you

When I needed someone to encourage me
I found support with you
When I needed someone to overlook my flaws
I found open arms with you
When I needed and wanted someone to love
I found my wish granted with you

With you the world is a beautiful place
With you I live among the stars
With you I explore the wondrous universe
With you I grow beyond myself

With you I can be what I am
With you I cherish each breath I take
With you I live and with you is life
With you I am one and feel complete

I was searching for a friend one day
The day I fell in love with you
Yesterday, today, and tomorrow
I am always in love with you

Whenever I'm Away From You

Time passes so slowly when I'm away from you
Time becomes meaningless whenever you're not near
Time passes so slowly when we are miles apart
Time allows me to think, lost time is my worst fear

Whenever I'm away, you're all I'm thinking of
Whatever I may do, I do to keep your love
Whatever I become, it is because of you
Whenever I enjoy success, I celebrate your love

Being apart is hard whenever I'm away
I miss all you are, you're such a part of me
Soon we'll be together renewing all our love
When you are in my arms time seems to melt away

Time passes so quickly whenever you are near
Time becomes meaningful when it is shared with you
Time becomes life itself just because you are here
Time and life stop whenever I'm away from you

The Gentleman and The Rogue

Many things about her are etched in my mind
So much to remember, unaffected by time
Moments long ago remain fresh today
So much to remember, never going away

Raised as a Gentleman and her as a Miss
Rogue wrestled conscience about that first kiss
Should I? Yes! No! What about.....If.....
They looked so soft, those luscious sweet lips!

That night Gentleman and Rogue made a bet
A decision once made I'll never regret
Neither piles of money nor stacks of chips
Could ever replace those luscious sweet lips

Now it's years later and we're still as one
Still kissing and loving as when we were young
Sometimes the Gentleman calls on the Miss
Sometimes it's Rogue demanding the kiss!

First kiss them together, then each one
Such a variety of ways, I'll never be done!
Many things were settled by answering that "if"
Both Gentleman and Rogue love those luscious sweet lips!

I Am

I am the symbol of the love you dream to live
I glisten and sparkle, reflecting the excitement of the union soon to be.
I am a perfect combination of the best the earth has to offer;
  Rare beauty, strength, refinement, and endurance.
I mirror the hope and anticipation of a fairy tale life recalled from the memories of
  childhood stories against the unknown realities just ahead
I embrace the warmth of one loving hand before becoming part of another.
I am perfect in the eyes of love, and am chosen to represent the vows of a
  lifetime
I am a reminder of that which God has created.

I am the witness to this life as one
  Multifaceted planes record for the memory, and replay upon demand with
  undiminished intensity.
I recall passion, anger, humor, and touch.
I reflect tears, smiles, joy and embraces.
I witness honesty, lies, hurts, and hugs.
I am a reminder of both good and bad.
I am only one, but symbolize the strength and the power of two in love.
I am the witness, and proclaim my history for all to see.

I am the symbol of a union that God has created.
I remain earthbound while love passes on.
  Though the hand no longer warms me, I still glisten and sparkle
  And reflect that which I have recorded to those who can still see.
I am the perfect combination of all that the earth has to offer.
I will remain as long as God creates.
I am Alpha meeting Omega.
I am your wedding ring
  And I remember.

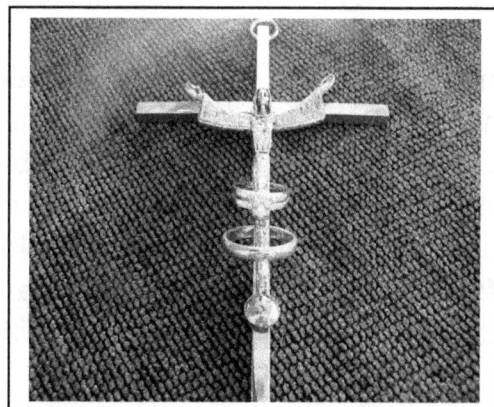

Signs

A sign outside our office points the way to the interstate highway. There is nothing unusual about this sign. Surely there are many thousands more all along these heavily traveled ribbons of pavement. Like its duplicates, it sits atop a wooden pole, impassively directing, unaffected by the elements. The shape is easily recognized, its colors reflecting bright whether illuminated by nature or man. Just doing its job, pointing the way. Such a simple thing!

Other signs do the same, although intended for different results. Some warn of potential danger, some command action. Some offer choices of food, lodging or fuel, while still more suggest places to visit, or places to rest for a short time. Some tell how far until the desired destination is welcomed into sight. All of them talk to us constantly, but do so silently, and without emotion. Just a sign on a stick, a mime without motion, directing.

We have become so accustomed to signs pointing the way that we scarcely recognize how important they are to us. We expect them to lead us to our desired location, and we follow them because our experience has shown them to be true. Go this way for this, and there it is! Go that way for that and you will find it. Amazing! That sign was right! Here I am, exactly where I wanted to be. Imagine that! I read the signs, even though I don't remember reading them... but knew if I read the signs and followed them, I would be where I wanted to be. The signs were true!

The signs are always there. Many times I am so familiar with my surroundings that the signs are unnecessary. Still they remain. Visitors are not so fortunate, for they may be passing this way for the first time. They seek the reassurance of the sign's directions, and comfort in the knowledge that the signs are true. If the signs are followed, they too will get to the place they desire. Just a sign on a stick, but earnestly sought by some.

In many years of driving, I have come to depend upon signs to direct me to my destination. Occasionally I miss one, and find myself somewhere other than where I want to be. The sign was there, directing, but I wasn't paying attention. I didn't see it. I didn't read it, but it was there. Too involved in myself, I passed by the sign, a chance to change direction, and reach my destination. Now I depend upon other signs to correct my course, and for them to be true. Others have paved and traveled this road before me, and thankfully, left these signs to help me find my way.

It's just a sign upon a stick, nothing unusual about it at all. It is a mime without motion, an impassive guide to my destination, placed by others who know the way. Such a simple thing, but only if I read the signs.

The Key

I have a key to his house.

The drive to Dad's is about three and a half hours, all on the Interstate. Driving alone allows a lot of time to think about the extent of his injuries, imagining the horror of the wound; the pain it must be causing; how quick-thinking Dad was to apply the tourniquet; how fortunate that a neighbor passed by when they did; wondering how much blood he'd lost; will he need transfusion?

I know why he was working alone.

That damned chainsaw! Dad had promised a neighbor that he would remove a stump in return for allowing him to cut down the deadwood for his fireplace. For some reason, the chainsaw became stuck as he cut the stump. I'm sure they all came into play...impatience, determination, irritation, self-imposed time restraints, fatigue...you can pick. He jerked. The saw roared, free from the stump, as Dad lost his balance. Just below the right knee, he rolled across the still turning chain. Thank God it wasn't the torso!

The truck was in the driveway as I pulled up to the house. I wondered who had driven it home. Everything was there: wood in the back; the crate with the oil and gas cans; a couple pairs of work gloves, the chainsaw.....and a small pool of blood just in front of the seat.

I have a key to his house. As I opened the door and stepped in, I stopped, and looked around. I was struck by the silence. No Dad smiling and greeting, happy to see me again. No hug. No smell of food simmering on the stove. No fire crackling in the fireplace. Nothing. Just the tick of the clock. Empty of what really makes that place home. As I brought my bags in from the car, that emptiness was replaced by warmth, because the more I looked, the more I saw of Dad. The beds were neatly made, the dishes all washed and put away, the tablecloth on the table just so. I gathered some of his clothes to take to the hospital. Socks on the left, underwear on the right, both in perfect tidiness. In the closet were slacks and shirts, already pressed, hangers evenly spaced. I smiled, and thought of myself.

I have a key to his house, but Dad is one of the keys to who I am.

I love you Dad, and I'm glad you are going to be just fine.

Hand in Hand

A daughter was born to a wonderful guy
She was born in the year in which Man learned to fly
He said, "Let's walk for awhile, there are many things to see."
Hand in hand, they walked for a way through history
What a remarkable time to live!

They saw still photos come alive through motion
The first World Wide War, what a commotion!
From working a farm with animal labor
To mechanical tractors and miles between neighbors
What a wonderful time to live!

The daughter grew up, married a wonderful man
And together they walked, hand in hand
Surviving prohibition and then The Depression
Another world wide war fueled by aggression
Still, a remarkable time to live.

Children arrive, and just as before
They walk hand in hand through tomorrow and more
From outhouse to in-house with considerable glee
From newspapers to radio and then to TV
What a remarkable time to live

Grandchildren are here and not any too soon
Flight has progressed from just yards to the moon
From horses directed by a tug on the reins
To mobile contractions with microchip brains
Still hand in hand a remarkable time to live!

Now in her nineties, the daughter, wife, mom and grandmother
Continues that history of walking with others
"Let's walk for awhile, there are many things to see.
Hand in hand we'll walk, and make more history!"
What a wonderful way to live!

You're Welcome

You're welcome is a lovely phrase
Wherever it is found
Surrendering smiles, goodwill, and praise
Sharing friendship and common ground

It's an answer to a thank you
The ending to a courteous deed
The beginning of timeless bond
So often given free!

It bids one "Come forward
Be not afraid
I will not discourage you
By the same hand we are made

To the early morning songbird
It's the response of the sun
With the symbol of a handshake
It's a friendship just begun

You're welcome means a lot to me
When found to be sincere
It means I've exchanged a memory
In the Brotherhood That Cares

Angel's Tears

The ways of Nature are often strange
So wide and varied in their range
Sometime excitedly and sometimes mild
I asked these questions as a child

Why does it rain in the middle of the day
And ruin the time in which to play?
Can't it wait to rain at night
While I'm indoors and out of sight?

Who controls the rain? I often wonder
And from where? Why does it thunder?
How can it rain when the sky is blue?
How does it know when water is due?

Sometimes I watch the sky become sad
Concealing its face with clouds, like hands
Tears begin falling, gently at first
Anguished now, Grief is the worst

As I have progressed throughout the years
I have come to view rain as Angel's Tears
Some spilt in sadness and terrible sorrows
On grief and heartache and lost tomorrows

Sometimes falling lightly in answer to a prayer
Bringing new life to that which was bare
Splashing against the hardness of Earth
They soften, combine, and offer new birth

Age answered questions youth eagerly sought
I witness the life these tears have brought
Gentle droplets have calmed my child hood fears
Now I view rain as Angel's Tears

Questions at 38

My experience tells me that the ability to scale the highest mountain is often found in the deepest valley. In the deepest valleys, the sun rarely shines, and it never warms. Cool darkness dominates all. Orientation is difficult. Is there more valley below me, or am I at the bottom now? I know I want to see the sun again, but the darkness hides success. Tired eyes search ahead for a sign of success, something I recognize, something positive I have experienced before.

Starved of confidence but not of determination, I move on, and still the valley withholds success. As success eludes, questions arise. Questions blind the eyes to the successes realized, and doubt steps forward. Doubt overwhelms confidence, but not the will. Will pushes the foot forward.

My experience tells me many things. It fails, however, to tell me where I am now. I know I dare not quit, for my life is not all that the valley may claim. There are others, whom I love, and they look to me for strength and guidance.

I must not fail.

I will move on.

Answers at 40

My experience tells me that the ability to scale the highest mountain is often found in the deepest valley. Though the darkness of the valley is lifting, I have not reached the top. Still I climb, sometimes slipping back. I try new paths, yet travel is slow and the trail looks long. Small successes along the way inflate their importance to my confidence, and strain to sustain it. Faith, in turn, grows to support success in its effort to feed confidence.

And that is the beauty of Faith. For it is in the depths and darkness of the valley that Faith is found, in small quantities or large, and where it's discovery becomes so important. Had it not been for Faith, I could not have looked down from the valley to view those mountain peaks I had scaled before, and thought were so high.

My experience tells me that the ability to scale the highest mountain is often found in the deepest valley. It has shown me not to fear the darkness of the valley, for that is where Faith is found. Faith restores vision to the eyes and sureness to the step, and will guide me to the light above the valley. My experience has shown me that perseverance and a simple Faith in God will overcome the Questions at 38.

He that believes is never alone.

And The Pendulum Swings

Alone again after several years
Tomorrow is hidden by a torrent of tears
Questions remain about what went wrong
While the clock continues its monotonous song
And the pendulum refused not to swing

Married too young, no foundation to last
Time to start over, get beyond what is past
The gingerbread house and white picket fence
Seen backwards through time never made sense
And the pendulum continues to swing

Avenging the hurt through multiple relations
Desperate for love, that lost revelation
No others understand this personal hell
As the hands creep towards the two o'clock bell
And still the pendulum swings

I want someone that will treat me right
Share the same values and live in God's sight
The embodiment of trust, great love and devotion
One who will erase all fearful emotion
I'm ready for the pendulum to swing

I want the freedom to share what I am given
To give what I get, a life worth living
Someone to support me as I support him
Just one for me, and only I for him
I need the protection of an angel's wing

I survived that broken dream of long ago
He, and time, has repaired my broken soul
The wounds have healed, there's no more bleeding
He allowed me to give to get what I'm needing
From within the protection of angel's wings

It took a long time but now I can trust
This character strength I've found is just
Free one again to love unreserved
I finally have found the one I deserve
Thank God the pendulum swings!

It's Not The Lies

It's not the lies that keep us apart
From seeing eye-to-eye, speaking the heart
It's not due to answers that seek to evade
Or phantom pressures that want to persuade
No, it's not the lies

It's not the lies about color or class
The slang, the strut or signs you flash
It's the way you look at me that I don't get
Angry for no reason, we've never met
It's something else, but not the lies

But had we traded lives for awhile
I might see why the face has no smile
It's the protection of anger offered by rage
Unwilling to crack, secured in the cage
This is the trouble, it's not the lies

Unloved at birth and less as a child
Untethered at home, allowed to run wild
Needing the unknown, seeking to belong
Success is infrequent, right becomes wrong
This is the trouble, it's not the lies

The inability to trust veiled in passionless eyes
Its history of disappointment just serialized
Frustrated at finding acceptance and love
The body now lies under the sterilized glove
This is the trouble, it's not the lies

HMS Incorporate

"Get more!" the Royals from the Kingdom of Profit once said
So Admirals summoned Captains to confer and eat bread
"The Royals require more than we have to give.
Go forth, procure, that they may prosper and live!"

The Captains went forth and admonished their fleet
"For the Kingdom to survive we will accept no defeat!"
First Mates went forth to outfit their ships
To accomplish that goal by persuasion or whips

To fill the ranks that the ships would need
Crews were assembled by deceit and greed
"A share in the spoils and holidays to rest!"
Right from the start words put to the test

Lured to work with promises and cash
Can't now remember when we saw family last
Experienced as officers in running a ship
We find ourselves now under the galley chiefs' whip

Once at sea there are no choices to make
Low pay and less benefits are booty to take
The Captain declares our plunder is lacking
"Up the count by four, the winds are now slacking!"

Though the Royals become richer, the masses do not
Life aboard Incorporate should not be our lot
Failed dreams and promises discourage the desperate
But life continues, on the HMS Incorporate

Saying Goodbye: Did I Do It Right?

The phone rang. It was Dad.

Before I even heard the words, I knew from his voice. Hope, now barely a flicker, had resigned to the inevitable. After nearly seventeen years of determined, courageous fighting against emphysema, Mom's strength was running out.

"Doc says I'd better call you boys. She doesn't have much time left." Dad said.
"We're leaving now." I replied.

It's a four-hour drive to the hospital, and we arrived around 11 PM. Everyone else was already there: Dad, my brother Todd, my maternal grandmother, Mom's sister, brothers, and others. Mom was very weak, but resting with the help of massive doses of morphine. Sometimes sleepily conscious, she seemed to recognize each of us. We were all there in support of her, but also in support of one another, for each of us was struggling to cope with that which was so near.

Dad paced, handcuffed with despair. He pleaded silently, unable to relieve her pain, unable to help, unable to do anything for her for the first time in over forty years. He memorized her face. He stroked her hair, whispered in her ear, kissed her forehead. And fought back tears.

Grandma kept her hands busy with crochet while she struggled within herself. Twice widowed, she had refused to face the loss of her eldest daughter. Although she possesses a deep faith in God, I'm sure she questioned Him continuously, wondering many whys.

Todd, always the one to mask his emotions, couldn't disguise the heartbreak in his eyes. She was the only woman he called Mother. She was the one to comfort him when the night terrors came. She was the one to whom he could tell his worst fears. She was the one who could help answer questions buried deep in the soul. She was the one who taught him what emotional love is all about.

I was by her when she surfaced to one of those foggy states of near consciousness. She tried to speak, but couldn't. I responded anyway, and I know she recognized me. She smiled. I held her hand and softly coaxed her to relax...and to let it go. I couldn't believe myself! I'm a monster! I was quietly and softly encouraging my mother to accept the end of this life! Never in her existence had she given up anything easily! Even this disease she had fought for so long and so courageously could not dampen her resolve to remain with us. And here was I, outrageously asking her to "let it go"! I prayed for God to end her suffering and to take her peacefully.

Mom endured that night and all the next morning, straining the last bubbles of oxygen from decimated lungs into an ever fading heart. Dad watched her breathe, finally calling for Doc when he saw no more. Doc came, checked her neck for a pulse, listened with his stethoscope. Looking at Dad, he shook his head and sadly said, "I'm sorry, Junior, she's gone." Instantly, tears and voice together poured out, anguished by the ending of a forty-two year love story few are lucky to know. I embraced my dad, and cried with him.

I had said goodbye, but wondered...Did I do it right?

Mom had always enjoyed getting "reading mail". From the time I went off to college through the end of her struggle, we exchanged news, events of our lives, thoughts and opinions on many things. Two or three days before she died, God inspired me to compose a prayer for her, and I had intended to share it with her while I could. I did bring it to the hospital with me, but could not summon the strength to read it to her. As we made final arrangements for Mom, I let my family read my prayer. Dad insisted upon including it in her service. I insisted that she take it with her, so now it lies in her hands for all eternity.

Not long after her funeral, I was alone at home one day and thinking of the many things we had done, times we had shared, and values she had taught me. It was a beautiful late summer day, and I was at peace with myself. As I watched the August clouds, I saw her face float by, eyes fixed upon something behind me that I could not see. Her expression was one of wondrous delight, and I realized that God had indeed answered my prayer.

A Prayer for Mom

O Lord God Almighty; Creator of Heaven and Earth and all Creatures therein; All-knowing Savior, Most Compassionate One; Loving Father unto which all must come.

So few of us of mortal soul seem to know the fullness of Your Love for each an every one of those created in Your Image. We fear the things we fail to understand or have not yet experienced. We look for answers, yet fail to see. We allow our fears to weaken our faith in Your ultimate love for us, and to question the trust that You require, the trust of a child in the love of his parents.

The love of a man for his wife, and of the wife for her man, grows ever stronger with the passage of the years. The strengths of the one support the weaknesses of the other as is Your intent. Through many trials of our earthly life, this love endures, and blossoms into a family. In turn, the family grows in love and faith, and again survives the trials of this existence.

And through it all, Your Love remains steadfast.

We of mortal existence must all face the end of this life. Again we fear that which we have not experienced. As strong as it is, the love and comfort of one for the other, and of the family for each other, must now give way to the Power and Grace of the Ultimate Love of God for the child.

This prayer for my mother is simple; that she see herself as a child of the Lord our Savior; that this love of such great power grant her a peaceful journey from this life into the next; and that she understands that the love of her family transcends this life, and accompanies her into the next.

Thank You, Lord, for hearing my prayer.

The Visit

My memory records Dad's mom as the first to go, followed a year later by his dad. The next one I remember is great Grandpa Ben, then Uncle Harvey, and my Grandpa Jack. My parent's friend Delos is there, as is great Grandma Rosa, Aunt Betty, Grandpa Charlie, Uncle Roger.

And my mom.

My wife's mom, Naomi, is there. Grandpa Gale and Grandma Fawn have their places too. Childhood friends and high school mates. The list goes on and on. And although they don't all reside in the same place, they are all together. I can visit anytime, they are always there, waiting.

I enjoy my silent visits, reminiscing of times past. Learning how to throw screwballs from my Grandpa Jack. The cherry smell of Uncle Harvey's pipe. Grandma Rosa's wonderful smile. Laughing at Delos' latest prank or retort. Watching Grandpa Gale work on cars in his garage and sneaking a peak at his calendar pin-up girls. Trips with Grandma Fawn to Paton for lunch, waiting for her to stuff the leftovers in her purse, and mentally calculating how many days it would be before she remembered them there. And the sheepish look in response to the teasing she took!

Marksmanship and woodworking with Uncle Roger, wine-making with Grandpa John. Casual conversations with Naomi through the screen door of her house. Never being too old for a kiss for Aunt Betty. Trips to California to stay with great Grandpa Ben and great Grandma Rosa, and visits to Disneyland! And that time as a toddler when Mom frightened me to hysteria by pretending to be angry with me, pulling a wig off her head and slamming it to the floor while yelling "You make me so mad I could just pull out my hair!" And then love and comfort me in earnest with hugs and kisses!

I enjoy my visits to their final resting places. Age and disease have exacted a price, and each of them have paid in full. But before leaving, these pillars of my life offered precious gifts. They taught me, encouraged excellence, made me feel important to them, and gave me their time. Beyond all that, they contributed more, by granting me a look at the many faces of love.

Go On

If I am now gone
The God has determined my earthly life done
If I have lived a Godly life
Then God offered the Good Lessons through me
If you watched me live and admired my ways
Then God taught you how to live

Go on, and live life as you were taught
Go on, and teach the way to live

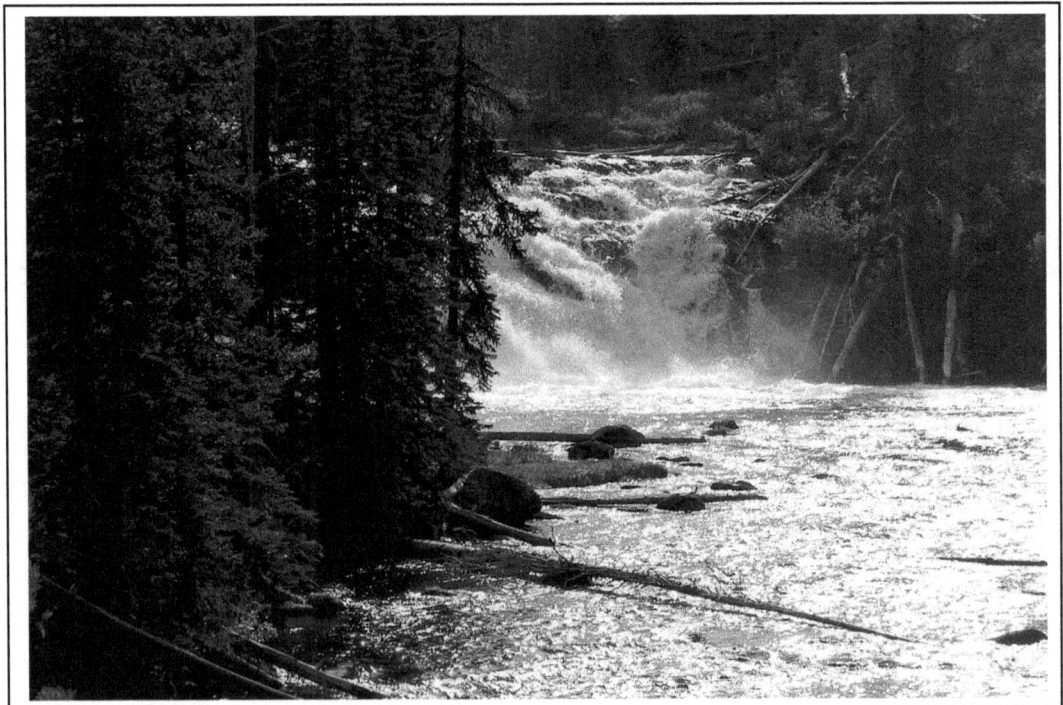

If I have lived a Godly life
And if you admired that life
And if you learned from that example
Then I have honored my responsibility to God

Go on, and live life as you were taught
Go on, and teach the way to live

It Was a Beautiful Day

It was beautiful that late October day
The blue autumn sky held all clouds at bay
A hint of crispness rode the breeze at play
Foretelling the promise of a perfect day
And I marveled at God's most beautiful day!

It was hard for my son to speak on the phone
He hesitated, trying to find strength in his tone
He pleaded, "Dad, can you please come home?"
At the news, the day's glory faded away
I no longer notice God's beautiful day

My flight chased the sun as it set in the West
Trying to catch it was my hopeless quest
In order to undo what this day had been done
A moonless night followed the setting sun
And darkness replaced God's beautiful day

That night's sleep came in tiny bits
Often punctuated by tearful fits
The same night greeted my new day rising
Nothing had changed, darkness still presiding
It was hiding God's most beautiful day

I felt that night would always be
A new day's sun I would never see
A late rising moon reflected His promise
Reminding me that He is never far from us
And that soon would be God's most beautiful day

I remembered that yesterday was a beautiful day
And that while I grieved God had not taken it away
It was I, not He, who had forgotten the day
For He had chosen my brother's day
And it was truly a most beautiful day

Once again a breeze rustled the trees
Whispering the sureness of a day that would please
A hint of light appeared in the East
A reminder that yesterday's beauty repeats
And announced the arrival of God's most beautiful day

I watched the sun slowly rise again
A glorious blaze of yellow burning
Triumphant over night in it's returning
Radiant in fulfilling God's promised ways
Of another of His most beautiful days

Building Paradise

Before my birth, Jesus told a story to me
Of His Children that were to be my family
He said "They are a faithful and obedient lot
Some with passions and tempers hot
Others subdued and tempers not
All very loving and caring for Me"

"While here their charge is to develop their talents
The choice is theirs, be it needles or mallets
Some choose the farm, others the city
All are hard workers, expecting no pity
Learning life's lessons from adversity
All very loving and caring for Me"

All become experts in their chosen field
All are bountiful in their yield
And Jesus is pleased as told by His smile
To me He said, "Go live for awhile.
In time all will return in single file
All very loving and caring for Me"

True to His Word, Jesus called Jergena one day
"Come on home, Jergena, come home to stay
I'm building Paradise, a most beautiful place
I want your help, there is much to be done
In order to be ready for the many and One"
So Jergena went home to prepare my way

Jesus called to John another day
"Come on home, John, come home to stay
I'm building Paradise, a most beautiful place
I want your help, there is much to be done
In order to be ready for the many and One"
So John went home to prepare my way

And so it was with Harvey and Jack
Later it was Betty, Paula, Ebie and Pat
Then there was Roger, Todd, and now Donnie
Be it singing or faith, needles or mallets
All my family is sharing their talents
They are building Paradise, and waiting for me

A Wailing in the East

From a distance, I hear wailing in the East
Carried by the wind, it fails to cease
A grievous cry of sorrow and loss
Begging answers from The Man Hung on the Cross

I hear wailing, coming from the East
Some people viewed important, some not the least
All shared a common, unplanned fate
All now have loved ones at Peter's Gate

I hear wailing, coming from the East
Having similar losses, I share their grief
Unknown to them, we shed common tears
After time and through Him, our eyes will clear

No mortal can comfort those in the East
Who's mournful cry is loss just released
Questions unanswered in this life remain
But viewed in the next become very plain

From a distance, I hear wailing in the East
Softer now, but still failing to cease
"Show them Grace" to Thee I pray
"Help them find strength for another day"

Far off in the distance it comes from the East
Carried by the wind to the most and the least
A message "Have Faith" addressing our loss
Direct from The Man Hung on the Cross

A Life Fulfilled

Life.

A word so simple, but of such profound and complex meaning that it sometimes defies adequate description. Yet defining it is exactly what each of us does with every breath we draw. People and events shape our lives, and contribute to our personal definition of life. Events, both positive and negative, weave a signature tapestry that we alone leave to those who remain behind. Powerful events trigger great emotional responses and become some of the strongest material of this life-tapestry.

Tragedy, unfortunately, is one of the most powerful events and a part of everyone's life. And when tragic events involve children, the effects seem multiplied many times. The ending of a new life is especially hard, stealing not only the life, but the dreams and hopes of and for that life now gone. New parents are robbed of watching the life conceived in love bloom into fulfillment. Siblings may always wonder "what if". Grandpa loses his connection to the future and a chance to begin life anew, while Grandma, armed with years of experience, has the joy of revisiting young motherhood snatched away. Friends, too, lose the opportunity to support the growth of another life into adulthood and its rightful place among others that survived.

But tragedy also provides opportunity, though not often seen through eyes blurred by tears of grief and sorrow. Friends and family offer support with embraces and sympathetic words. The most comforting words have been around for a long time, and often find voice in times of tragedy. One such tragic event, that of a stillborn boy, perfect of body but unable to sustain life, provide an opportunity for one friend to support another with these words:

God's plan is often misunderstood by us when we strive to put reason where we think it should be. He tells us "All will be revealed" at the proper time and in the proper place. "Have Faith, and Trust in Me" He says, and yet we hear not, our logic and emotions overpower the quiet patience of Faith. Grief demands to be heard above all else. Faith understands, and waits to comfort after Grief tires and fades away.

Whether life on this Earth is long or short, it is the gift of the Holy Spirit that makes us who we are, and is the one thing that transcends from this life into the next. Surely, God's plan was for you to see and to hold His creation. But at this time, and in this place, His is the greater need. As each of us reach that time to transcend, our spirit will join those passing before us in joyous understanding of God's plan, and of a life fulfilled.

It's Time

I remember the times
Many years ago it seems
Of walks in the park, talks on the bench
And of confiding in you and the trees

I remember the times
Much later as I recall
Again you were there in my time of need
To absorb the blow or break the fall

Whenever I was down
Yu would reach out to me with praise
You words encouraged a saddened heart
To rise above my malaise

And in my exuberance of celebrating success
When I had forgotten your presence
You patiently waited, knowing I would return
And finally acknowledge your influence

It's time for me to reflect upon my life
And on those who have played a role
It's time to take stock
And look at the whole

It's time to seek your presence
Not only in the park or on the bench
Or when I fall or become discouraged
Bur daily, my thirst only you can quench

It's time to acknowledge your gifts of love
And begin to repay in kind
To give others encouragement and praise
And to use wisely the gracious gift of time

Seasons of the Mind

Age allows discovery of many things I find
Seeing, feeling, using senses of all kind
From what tastes good and what is hot
To learning phrases for that which I want
And such is the infant season of mind

Childhood builds on the infant behind
Bedtime is still way before nine
Toys and TV are primary diversions
Books and tales unlock grand illusions
As I pass childhoods season of mind

Youth arrives and finds me outdoors
Playing, climbing, wandering to explore
By experience I discover walls to my universe
Then sometimes for better, sometime for worse
Reality arrives… and now I have chores!

The seasons of life continue on
Through teens, the twenties and then beyond
Youth fades away while maturity creeps in
Strange new concepts form from within
More seasons of the mind with which to bond

Seniority stands in the life behind
Bedtime returns to way before nine
Childhood acquaintances dwindle in number
Photos and tales speak of times to remember
As I pass Grandpa's season of mind

Age allows discovery of many things I find
Those I treasure most are by Heavenly Design
I learn material things matter not up above
Unlike Kindness, Faith, and most of all Love
And such is my current season of mind

Age allows discovery of many things I find
From the simplest of those to the truly divine
Childlike, I must return to that place
In the hope of receiving His merciful grace
And begin anew the seasons of the mind

Where The Sky Ends

It invites a look, this sky up above
Just out of my reach, but not from The Dove's
Sometimes stretching out way beyond sight
Childlike, it teases my physical plight
The Body, aware of its limits by design
Passes the questions on to The Mind

When distance limits the ability to see
The Minds takes over from the physical me
"Where does it end?" The Mind wants to know
"A finite place! It must be just so.
I'll create the tools with which to find."
These are the thoughts of The Logical Mind

The Mind is not satisfied with earthbound feet
Creatively assuring gravity's defeat
A Mind not satisfied with limited vision
Created telescopes, extending its mission
Still not satisfied, The Mind yearns for more
Always returning to the lessons before

The Truth has been told since Time first began
When Man was created from humus and sand
When The Mind can not explain where the sky is at end
It always awakens the slumbering friend
The Mind becomes aware of its limits to know
And thus passes the question on to The Soul

The Soul know the answers The Mind can not find
It speaks to The One who created all kind
Concepts like Faith, Hope and Love it defines
Not limited nor daunted by cerebral confines
Body and Mind question where the sky ends
"Your answer confused, please tell us again"

The Mind also asks, "What happens after death
When the Physical Body uses no breath?"
Kind Soul, once again, tries to explain
But to The Body and Mind it just isn't plain
What The Body and Mind can not comprehend
Is known only to The Soul, and Where The Sky Ends

Safe Haven

Living life creates opportunities
For you to handle as you please
Some responses offer difficulties
Some solutions come with ease

Living life creates situations
Where you can determine your role
A decision full of reflections
Revealing the passions of your soul

Demands on your time
Pressures to produce
Depression is on the line
Desperation a tightening noose

When your burdens become too much
When life confronts you head on
When all others are out of touch
You need just one to depend upon

And when you have lost your way
Ask for safe haven here
Seek safe haven here
Come to safe haven here

Share your troubles with me
For you are My Child
And I have a special love for thee
Accept safe haven here.

The Twinkle in My Eye

The topic of conversation is so typical
That I feel the need to seed my discretionary agenda
To your hollow demeanor

I play on your ego like lady luck does cards
And pluck at your heart strings like Mao to a sold out crowd
I take little curtsies and bows in gratitude

Ignorance is bliss, but please understand
I do not exploit your child-like mind for dominance or gain
But simply for the pleasure of the game

Logistically placed pawns
On the plane of your periphery
Check mate

My Confession

I thought I knew

I was mistaken
I know nothing of you and you of me

I gave my heart to you that night
A fool's treasure delight
And cast away my soul

Even though I know it was bold
I gave you my most precious possession
And yet, no affection

A glance here and there, are you checking to see if I'm still there?
I try to hide, but I can't deny
The pain I feel now that you're not here

I'll tell you now
I'll never wear a crown
I'm not 5 foot 2 and blond with blue

I'm fatty and round
And completely brown
I can't hide that fact, believe me, I've tried

I just don't understand, was it that I was then and this is now?
And there's no one else to fall back on?
You had to settle for second best?

My confession:
I can't help my conception
But I've tried to change in discretion

I wasn't born with a figure
So I tried to create one out of vigor
But my attempts went unconfigured

The Truth:
I guess I'm not the one for you
I didn't come from a box or a set of two

The only thing I can divulge
Is my undying love for one
And hope it will be justifiably won

Tainted World of Glitter

The fight that I lead
Is the cure for the disease of
Hopeless materialism
That infects all the mamas and papas
Who lay their sleepy children to bed on pillows of wanderlust
This fascination with metals, silks and gold
Leads me to believe
That the addiction of wanting
Has overcome the desire to please
This hopelessness to fight the Tyrant on the 92nd floor
Sees its image on the floor
In platinum-laden figurehead
That costs more than a poor farm hand's sweat and tears
Throughout his many tough years
You Sir
With the thousand dollar suit and golden tassels
The gleam in your eye is no longer pride
But the rollover of another dollar into your bank account
And the cracks that you hear
Comes from the backs of the people you walk on
But the gleam that you see steam from his eyes
Is the sweat from another back-breaking day
And a solitary tear for the pain

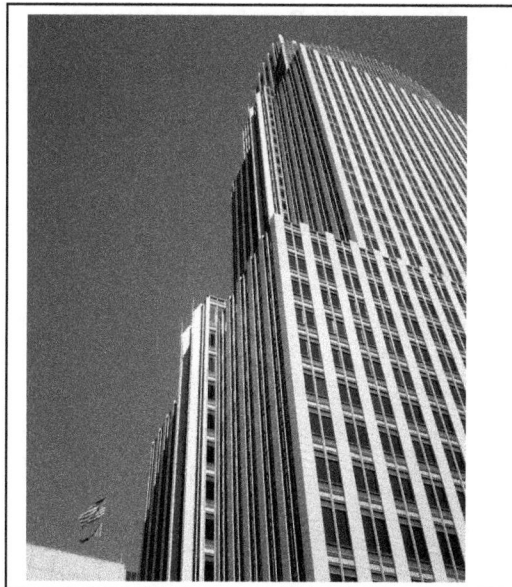

Expressions of Undying Love in the Dead Form

The fading petals of love arrive to find
An oasis awaits encased in glass

The veins, with a svelte touch
Pump bright life into the heart of time

In elaborate detail and divine design
They flock together to showcase their fine lines
Against the backdrop of crepe paper

Intertwined with ribbons and lace
They light up the face
That comes in to steal its heavenly nectar of amore

The aroma that protrudes
Links the two
In an everlasting dance between skylight and night

Too soon these floral cupids of desire
Shoot their last arrows through the heart of love
And decline into fragile crepe paper hearts

Their souls lay bound between the letterhead and binding
To be given life again in the withered hands of time
A long-travelled sailor on the sea of passion and pride

Rising Tide

The water is high
Yet the tide keeps rising

I float just long enough to think
Before I finally start to sink

And still the tide rises

All the forces in the world
Could not save me from this undertow

I feel its cold, clammy grasp
As it pulls me asunder

I wait for a sign
A rescue boat of some kind

Too little, too late
A seemingly sealed fate

And still the tide rises

As I go, down below, I still wait in wonder
For some kind of blunder

Some act of fate
That will take my place

And still the tide rises

Oh God!
What could I have done to deserve such a dire fate?

This hate you breed towards me
Lingers and breathes for me here in the depths

But it waits out my battle cry in vain

Check Please

Folly is all my attempts
To secure some sanctity and repents
For I am just one of many sheep

Drowning on your deceit
Falling at your feet
Asking for a receipt
So that I may return your lies full heap

I have committed my crimes
And have done my penance in full

So I ask You now, Almighty
What the staff is for in time of crisis?

If what they say is true
Then grant me this last reprieve
If my plight is one of dreary

Then take the one thing I hold dear
And give it to someone near
And pray that they are the wiser

Line in the Sand

Lines will be drawn in the sand
Between the hourglass and our hands

Dunes as far as the eyes can see
With seemingly insurmountable odds
Spaced between dreams

We walk the desert floor in search of something more
A private oasis hidden from the fury of the land
Where happy idleness takes the form of outstretched canopies over sand
In the shadows of the Promised Land

The journey, however, will be arduously long
Filled with peril, delusions, blunders and hind sights

Each started their own journey with one set of footprints in the sand
But atop a foreign land
Our soles intertwined because of fate's hand in time
And somewhere along the line, our souls combined
That's the first time we crossed the line

The journey continues onward with two shadows cast upon the land
Hand in hand, we glide atop the mountain of sand
Fighting the quicksand of trepidation that comes with your life's plan
Now comes the time to contend with another line

Duty and time have created this line
The crime of indecision boggled my mind
But the borders are too vast to feel the warmth of your smile
So I will cross the line
And follow you blind

Because it's all just a matter of time
Before you will be forced to contend with the line
And make time to find our place in the sky
Where love's immortality takes the form of two stars aligned
Showing our journey's horizon now at the door
As we each take stock in the valley floor

And will you cross the line, or stay behind?

Not everyday will have the perfect sunrise
Nor will we always share a sunset

But I promise to cross the line, not even blind
And walk with you through the valley shadows
And the sunshine for all time

So long as your hand and your heart are mine

Divide and Conquer

If all this was to you was a game of divide and conquer
Then I'm at your mercy
My white flag is showing
Mark my ruins with yours

I idly sit and wait as you decide my fate
No deliberation to be had
I'm check-mated out
With my sword stuck in the sand

I should be the captain on the hill pondering your estate
But still I wait below
In the dark and gloomy valley
As you sit upon your throne tossing coins

Wading out into the abyss
Suddenly finding myself taking unnecessary risks
Good luck with future conquests
I'm in need of bed rest

Little Hide-Away in the Hills

The bustling lights of the city
The sounds of cars heading to unknown destinations

Headlights look like fireflies tonight

Motion in every direction
Yet the destination remains the same
Looking down upon this ocean of sparkling lights with awe
Mere words can not describe this place

It's magnificence only outdone by its beauty

I retreat to this place of solitude high upon the hills
Away from the noise and lights

The sheer chaos of life

This place, mere brick and stone, gives so much more
A chance to breathe and regain my balance
And get back my sense of time
Time that seems lost or left behind

Back in the city of bustling lights

Here I can regain my perspective and composure
For I am just one of millions in this star-lit blanket

Twinkling now and again in the crisp night sky

A reminder of how small everything in life really is
You are just one light
One star in the scheme of things
Too little to do it alone, but big enough to shine

And add color to the otherwise shadowed night
Hidden in the bluff, I watch life in the city pass in a glimpse
Red flares adorn our keeper

A single high-rise in the center of this small universe

Watching over her inhabitants
She symbolizes all that is the viewed world
And time itself
She bellows, piercing the night sky

Calling all home to the madness of city life

Where time is lost between the cracks of city streets
And souls are left to wander

It's easy to see where life begins and ends
Where souls are lost or saved
When the bustling city lights give way
To the prowling night and into existence

Fighting Shadows

Fighting shadows of a previous existence
They follow me into the night
Persuading me to the left or right
My demons are persistent and to the point

"Follow me into the night
And the shadows and the fright
Follow me where there is no path
And where no grass grows
Follow me down where there is no end
And thus no beginning
Where there is no sense of time or place"

Time exists
But is not present
It prevails
But is not pertinent
Ambiguous, yet static
All is as it is and will always be
We are neither here nor there

But somewhere in between fighting shadows

Pursuit

Slicing though the weary night
A soul searches for its guiding light
Casting shadows on the ground
It searches only to be found

The life we lead between the lines
Leaves pages full of empty ramblings
Like those of a blind man
Who searches for something he can never see
A man without purpose
Is a poet without words
Blank pages in the rushing current of time
Trivial pursuits for happiness or despair
Any feeling to secure a beating heart
An open prayer passes through these lips to the floating air
Carried on the winds of optimism
Awaiting an attentive ear to beseech its requests
Waiting for a response
Any sign that someone else can feel the pain
That resonates within these walls

Slicing through the weary night
A soul searches for its guiding light
Casting shadows on the ground
It searches only to be found

Journeys in May

In grade school
I counted down the days to summer
And measured time in innings of baseball games
Never wanting the sunset to find me

In middle school
I counted down the days between dances and my chances come May
And measured my time in puppy-love crushes and detention time
Searching for acknowledgement in the shadows of self-doubt

Then in high school
I counted down the days to May and graduation day
And measured my time in boyfriends, kegs and soccer games
Relieved to never again follow a foreign timetable or schedule

Now in college
I count down the days to the beginning of the rest of my life
And measure my time in giggles and smiles from those fading away
Eager to start their own journeys in May

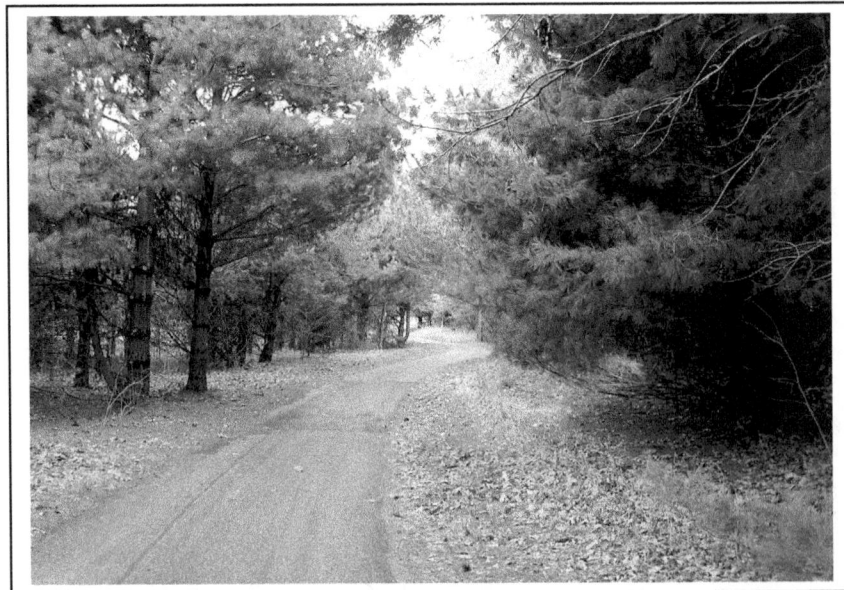

9/11

The paper is empty
There are no words to capture what 12 did to millions
They'll rot in hell for their crimes
But what about their victims?
They will never see another sunrise
First Steps
Graduations
Wedding days
Retirement age
Cut down by terror
But instilled with courage and hope
Their bodies are gone
But their souls and their stories
Are immortalized in the dusted footprints of the two towers
That now lay between their loved one's feet
And on the same day two years later
We hear stories of your courage and of your loss
We honor you in silent prayers
And wait for your response
We love you

Look No Further

When life fills you with sadness and despair
When you feel your light begin to fade
And your faith begin to fail
Take a look around
See what gave you life

The moon gave way to the sun once more
The horizon held it with affection
Nature smiled at her beauty
Everything awoke in her warmth
The waves rolled in once more
The tides beat against the shore, polishing the rocks
The blades of grass that gave you life
Grew from her warmth and love
The water you drink came from her blue bosom
And when you die
You will become one with the rich soil
And become a blade of grass
Or a grain of wheat
You will become a drop of water in the ocean
And a whisper in the wind
You will help the next generation to see the sun rise